BRIDGING THE
GAP

BRIDGING THE
GAP

PARTRIDGE

To order additional copies of this book, contact
Toll Free 800 101 2657 (Singapore)
Toll Free 1 800 81 7340 (Malaysia)
orders.singapore@partridgepublishing.com

www.partridgepublishing.com/singapore

Contents

Acknowledgements

Thank you to my parents who have patiently been supporting me through the entire process. Thank you for giving me the freedom to curate my path and for providing me a home.

Thank you to my brother who is always so encouraging and for believing in me. I am grateful for all of your support, especially during the struggles.

I would like to express my gratitude to my, facilitator, lecturer, Christopher Jabines, who went through my topic of research and provided valuable guidance for the research.

I am also blessed with an incredible bunch of friends who have been with me throughout this journey. It was for their faith in me that motivated me to finish writing the book. My friends are integral to my happiness and success over the past couple of years. Thank you so much my IJ girls and MI friends.

Thank you to Ri Chang for giving me guidance for this book during its initial stages and providing me with valuable advice.

Thank you, Joan Kabche and Eunice Salinas for contributing to this book. I have learned so much from the both of you in Romania. You girls made my summer 15 an amazing one. Thank you for believing in me.

Thank you to everyone else who have showered me with kind thoughts and blessings. Thank you from the bottom of my heart.

Introduction

I will call it a blessing to have had dropped out of junior college at a vulnerable age of nineteen. I made the decision solely based on my intuition. I did not have to ask an astrologer or even consult my parents who were my providers. I knew it was a massive risk, but I assumed it was the way of the universe. It was the way of waking me up to take a deeper look at the current model of education and see what is missing.

I had quickly come to a realization that I was part of the glorified rat race. It had kept me feeling stuck. I often felt inadequate. I was always competing against others. I never really was satisfied with what I was achieving in school or college.

In school and college, I was considered the average Joe. Most teachers use to regard me as a mediocre student. We live in a society where we take external validation too seriously that I use to believe in them without a doubt. The grades I had attained in school determined my self-esteem.

How did I then break out of the shell?

It was when I was on a study break mid-2014. It was also the darkest days of my life. Most of my relationships were messed up. Both my mental and physical health was deteriorating. I was cursing the world for what it had done to me. I was regretting who I have become. Long story short, I was drowning in a victim mentality.

However, through all of this, there was a voice inside of me that kept saying things would get better. How cliché you might think. I did not have a better option, so I decided to obey it. Amidst the negativity, I stumbled upon self-help books. I then went on to spend all my days in the library reading on the concepts of healing.

The further I immersed myself in this pool of knowledge that I had never encountered, the more I started understanding new concepts such as mindfulness practices and happiness.

I soon realized that I was not the only individual going through pain and suffering. I was not the only one depressed over my life. I knew many others who have gone through it and have dealt with it efficiently.

I am a natural when it comes to mediating. Hence problem solving was in my DNA. I quickly was now trying to think of ways to save the world when I was just cursing it months earlier. I know the irony. Have a good laugh and carry on reading.

I started doing more research, and I came to a conclusion that we needed a more humanistic approach to solving the issues that students face. I figured that it was not that we had to create more drugs to prescribe or innovate new disorders. What we have to do is trace back to the roots of the problem. The approach we have to take is much simpler than we can imagine.

Our current education system is missing a key element, and that is spirituality. Spirituality often gets a bad rep of being somewhat a mystical fantasy. Hence I think it is essential that we break down this broad concept. Spirituality is innate a sense of connection to something more than our physical beings. It usually comes up when there is a search for meaning in our life. Spirituality links to a purpose. A spiritual journey is often personal, that being said it is mainly about personal growth in aspects of life. It is not just about knowing an idea or belief but more of the acting upon what we know. It allows the freedom of one to think of ideas and ways to progress in life. Hence any activity that helps you grow as a person can be considered a spiritual experience. Spirituality began about 60 years ago after World War 2 where people started falling out of religion. This is key to realise that religion is very different from spirituality.

Religions on the other hand are schools of limited thoughts and beliefs. It was crafted in the times when science was absent to make it easier for people to understand their existence. Spirituality promotes a universal consciousness and the potential to master your inner self. Thus you can see that spirituality defers from religion and is accessible to all human beings on the planet.

In psychology (note that I will be using a lot of references from psychology as I did study psychology at the end of my search for inner peace) we learn that are multiple bits of intelligence present in human development.

Multiple bits of intelligence include cognitive, emotional, moral, kinesthetic, personal, aesthetic and spiritual. I feel that there has not been much emphasis placed on spiritual knowledge in school. I can even safely say that most of us are spiritually weak.

Spirituality could help people wake up to the actual reality to become conscious and aware of their surroundings. In fact, spirituality can be very practical and to infuse it into the education system is much needed.

I believe it is my calling to share my thoughts on this to the educators of the world or just anyone who believe in education to look deeper into the framework they have built for our current students. I completed this book after my travels around the globe. Having worked and interacted with internationals have helped me gain more perspectives towards the education system on a global scale. I have therefore gathered some insights and included it in here. I also conducted a study on standardized testing and education. I have shared the research in this space.

Chapter 1
The Gap

There are few gaps that schools are yet to patch. We live in the age of generation Y. Schools are still teaching them history and geography that are now easily, obtained by the touch of our advanced computation devices. I then think it is a waste of time and resources. The mind of an individual is evolving from time to time so is the technology and the world around us. That is evident to us, for instance, take your mobile gadget, it has transformed through the years what started out as a gigantic piece of structure to an all- encompassing touch screen revolution. Hence it is necessary for our education system to develop into a transformation model that will help students to reach further heights and potentials.

The school is less concerned to teach real life issues that can hold back one from living a genuinely satisfying life. Education must shift from feeding us information to teaching us how to live extraordinary lives. We are in a world full of possibilities. We have people flying back and forth to the moon and why is it that we still teach students history that does not help them in the present moment. Sure there might be a great inspiration one could look up to through history but just by regurgitating the facts and details on an exam paper and grading it to qualify them for their lives sound absurd.

The first gap is between the skills one necessarily need and how much exposure they receive. With real issues, schools must be teaching mindfulness practices, nutrition, and health, relationship skills, teaching them the basis of happiness that it comes from within.

We must teach them the art of nurturing. We need to show them how they can empower their minds to set sustainable goals. I mean to show them something that will help in the long term.

We have to teach them adequately something that is worth knowing. Information and facts about geography and history are not going to cut it. Those are already available to them through the mother of Internet, Google.

We must teach our generation to dream big. We do not need students to copy material from Wikipedia into their school projects. We need to instill courage over fear in our students to rebuild faith in humanity.

The lessons taught in school by teachers are lacking arousal to stimulate the minds of students. The lack of stimulation then hinders the ability for students to naturally assess and ask inquisitive questions. I remember vividly how whenever one of our teachers tries asking us questions after a lesson, the only deafening response would be still silence.

Schools must stop domesticating students and start giving them the freedom and time to think and create what they desire as no two human beings are alike. It astonishes me as to how schools can subside to conformity when we are all born with different talents to offer.

Schools must also stop judging students based on the grades they have attained. According to Popham (1999), standardized testing performance should not be the basis to rate the character of education. The underlying reason why the grades attained is not a true indicator of educational efficacy is because any assumption about educational aspect with regards to the achievement in standardized testing is considered irrational.

For several important reasons, standardized achievement tests should not be used to judge the quality of education. The overarching reason that students scores on these tests do not provide an accurate index of educational effectiveness is that any inference about educational quality made on the basis of students standardized achievement test performances are apt to be invalid. It helps us identify that standardized testing does not equate to education.

Popham (1999) also reported that if one spends enough time with the language of the content which is the way it is described, given in the guidebooks that come together with standardized achievement tests, one will be able to identify what is tested are often reasonably familiar. There is a need for generalization in the descriptors so that the educators of the nation who might have a varied curriculum could accept it. Those descriptors need to be general to make the tests acceptable to a nation of educators whose curricular preferences vary. However, the generalized use of descriptions of what is being tested usually allows inferring the arrangement of teaching testing, which is disoriented.

In addition to the discrepancy that whether acknowledged or ignored will usually result in phony conclusions about the efficacy of education in a particular setting if the grades attained on standardized achievement tests are used as a measure of the quality of education. Thus that should be the very reason why it cannot be a determinant of testing the effectiveness of a nation, school or teacher. It is almost a certainty that there is a compelling discrepancy between what is taught in the classroom and what is tested in the examination. (p.8-15). This portion clearly shows how standardized testing is too generic to be of substantial value. As mentioned in the results, most examination follows a rhythm attuning to similar phrasing of questions and answers that have been prepackaged for students.

This is evident from the endless number of past examination papers that a student practices year after year. Moreover the generic nature is only able to produce students with average capacity like what the results indicate. This practice may help one to do well in the examination but whether it stretches the true potential of one is highly a doubt.

While reviewing other literature, I was able to find more about standardized testing. In illustrating the rationale behind the effects of standardized testing, Campbell (1976), developed a law that states achievement tests may be a beneficial measure of ordinary school achievements under circumstances of regular teaching aimed at ordinary competence. But when it is all that matters, they both lose their worth as measures of educational dignity and deceive the educational development in unpleasant ways.

In addition to that research, we have the headmaster of ETON college that is based in England, who mentioned in an interview "We compound the problem by having an unimaginative exam system, little changed from Victorian times, which obliges students to sit alone at their desks in preparation for the world in which, for much of a time, they will need to work collaboratively." Sky News telecasted this interview. If a headmaster could understand the current situation and question the value of the system, I think it is the time we as educators stop lying to ourselves that the ancient method will help our millennial live an extraordinary life.

On top of that, have you wondered why one has to spend so much on tuition? Why must one go to the end of debt just to get an average paying job? Why the need to process loans and bonds when the result is debt and stress? Countries like Norway, Sweden, and Germany, offers tuition-free universities. Hence it is only fair for countries with high GDP to give all a chance to pursue higher education.

In contrast, we see people who are prosperous and happy. Many of them proudly label themselves as dropouts and that they have quit college. Situations as such can make one feel even more depressed as they do not understand why they have to go through the arduous route to reap limiting benefits.

What I have led to found is the gaps in the architecture of our system. Popham (1999) states that the companies that create and sell standardized achievement tests are all owned by large corporations. Like all for-profit businesses, these corporations attempt to produce revenue for their shareholders. (p. 8-15). It helps us understand that there is an imbalance in the system as education is a profit generating industry. This profit earning mindset of the system then does not provide an authentic learning experience for students as it merely prepares them only to do well in standardized tests, which is flawed in nature. Popham (1999), reported that the creators of these tests act outstandingly in determining test items that are anticipating to amount all of the material's knowledge and skills that are regarded vital by the educators of the nation.

However, the test planner is having difficulties putting it to task. Hence, it becomes a constant that standardized achievement tests will contain many items that are not regulated with what's accentuated pedagogically in a specific setting. (p.8-15). These results show that there is a gap between the realities of what should be conducted and what is being conducted.

I believe we are souls of purpose and enlightenment. We are here to create a better planet and build a stronger humanity. We are not here to be greedy money mongers to destroy the earth. There is a reason why many issues are rising like climate change and poverty. There is no way issues of the above can compare with the problems of the system. But such matters will not be resolved if the systems do not change.

Mainly, the education system, which is supposed to produce people who must preferably be eliminating such causes. One good instance was the rejection of a vegan activist, Gary Yourofsky to give a lecture in a school in Israel.

It happened as the teacher from the school mentioned that his message was too "scary" for the students in school. It was rather funny to hear that as it sounds like the teachers are not willing to let students listen to the truth of the industries. The cruelty and discrimination taking place in the meat, dairy and egg industry.

The school has to raise awareness of such issues. The label of being vegan may sound like an extreme one. However, it is the simplest solution towards issues such as world hunger, environmental degradation and health related diseases and conditions. I am well aware that this book is about the gaps and the solutions geared towards the education system. Do not fret. I am not writing or preaching against veganism. That topic needs a book and space of its own. However the fact that a school will not allow for such great knowledge to enter is quite unbearable.

Our culture has cared and encouraged the development of the left-brain. The left-brain characteristics are so well conditioned to believe that one must go about their entire life trying to achieve and accomplish. The left-brain is only capable of behaving rationally and analyzing just about everything that is taking place. However, rationalization in nature itself is a defense mechanism employed by the ego to defend one against conflicts and anxieties by neglecting unpleasant thoughts and impulses to the unconscious.

Hence there is clearly a level of submissive behavior rooting due to pressure from society that school and college are the only way to success. This consistent behaviour of us satisfying the left-brain characteristics has led to the trauma of chronically disabling the right-brain characteristics. It also means that we are thinking too much and doing things in a frenzied fashion. Thus, causing us to have not had time.

After all, we are known as human being. We could have only been called human doing if all we are concerned with is what we are thinking and doing all the time. It is a pity, as we are not trained well enough to tap into our right brain that could help flow in regards to creativity, holistic thoughts, intuition, and skills. To further understand let us get an insight of what goes on in the right brain.

It is the part of the brain where all strings are loosely attached. It is the portion where it is more relaxed than the left-brain that readily accepts visual information, which is ready to be guided through natural intuitive information. It pretty much has the capability to see the bigger picture in any scenario present. It is also the side of the brain which no doubt is more creative than the left-brain. By engaging our right brain, we also activate the parasympathetic nervous system.

More parasympathetic motion means less stress and hence improved health. Many doctors including Dr. Andrew Weil suggests that engaging in spiritual activities can achieve such movement. I'll share more about the spiritual activities in the later chapters.

The right brain also does not have the control freak edge as compared to the left-brain in which activates the adrenaline releasing sympathetic system. However, my concern is that we are clearly not programmed to master the right-brain characteristics in schools. Many do not even understand the term intuition. Many even think that intuition sounds far off, as they are so accustomed to the rituals and patterns of the left-brain. Research has shown time and time again as to how meditation can change the neurology of the brain and strengthen the functioning. So why are such vital practices not part of the framework of schools? Sure in the recent times some schools may have adopted the practice of meditation. One excellent example will be Visitacion Valley Middle School in

San Francisco. Introducing a meditation programme in 2007 in the school had helped reduce suspension rates by 45%. Thus it must be implemented on a bigger scale across the globe.

The issue then is the fact that modern education has worked to master the practical abilities of the left-brain that causes an imbalance. Therefore, one just goes by their day-to-day lives ignoring right brain's intuition, concealing their emotions. Our fast paced life has also immensely contributed to discarding our use of the right brain as we are in a world that floods us with so much information that it is not that we do not have the answers to a great life.

It is the fact there are too much information and too little time to process the load of information resulting in failure. This high dosage of information from different mediums causes students to be highly distracted. It then becomes a barrier for students to pay attention to lessons taught in school.

However, psychologists have come up with a reason to believe that this failure of the focus of students could be due to ADHD. It has led to pills and potent drugs prescribed. It can cause more harm at the end of the day. Drugs can only be used to treat the symptom. For us to address the cause, we have to dig deeper.

We are in a world where notifications bombard us almost every minute of the day. Take the smartphone for instance, with so many redundant notifications and emails that we barely have time to engage in things that matter. We think it is serving our needs quickly. But the aftermath is reflected at a later stage when we get caught in mental stress and even illness.

We need a system whereby we are allowed to teach students on how they can tap into their inner guidance system to face challenges. Also on how they can efficiently release negative emotions and thought patterns. Let me share with you a story. I used to think that disease is foreign to the body and that there was no clear explanation. However, I stumbled upon Louise Hay's work and everything made sense to me.

Louise Hay, a pioneer in the field of psychoneuroimmunology, a scientific study of how emotions impact your immune system defines disease as merely the suppression of thoughts and feelings. The more negative the feelings, the more conditions to attract. Every emotion has a vibrational frequency and energy. We all know from basic science that energy cannot store in your body. It requires movement. Suppressing it or trying to control your anger for instance only deprives your body of energy that could ideally work for essential activities.

Thus it is crucial to enlighten students with knowledge of how they could physically get rid of negative emotions and thoughts. It is not only a healthier way to guide the students; it is scientifically proven to be effective in the behavior of students.

It has become a norm for schooling teenagers to pick up the habits of smoking and drinking. Some even go to the extent of consuming drugs. Drugs contain a chemical that could communicate with the brain's communication system, and it distorts the brain's natural chemical messengers by over arousing the interest of the 'reward circuit' of the brain. Why the need to fondle with the 'reward circuit'? Could it just be for the thrill or is there an underlying root problem that has been left unaddressed? We cannot let loose as the concern of this issue accumulates day by day and the faster we diagnose the better will be the rate of good health for our generation Y.

Students pick up such habits to feel intoxicated, to relieve their mental stress and even to have the energy to work harder. Ever wondered when did all these stress and lack even started to take control of an individual's life? We were all once happy little children, and life did not just happen. That is the lie that we are all let to believe.

In fact, most of us immerse in this lie. We have allowed it to consume us leading to misery. One of the main concepts that our modern education is missing out on will be coaching more EQ, also known as an emotional qualifier that regards to our abilities into perceiving, controlling and expressing our emotions.

It was Peter Salovey and John D. Mayer who invented the term 'Emotional Intelligence' in 1990. They described it as "a form of social intelligence that involves the ability to monitor one's own and others' feelings and emotions, to discriminate among them, and to use this information to guide one's thinking and action". EQ can refer to complexity management in three important ways.

First, individuals with lower EQ are less capable of handling stress and anxiety. Since complex situations are equipped and challenging, they are likely to induce pressure and stress, but high EQ acts as a buffer. Second, EQ is a key ingredient of interpersonal skills, which means that people with higher EQ are better equipped to navigate complex organizational politics and advance in their careers.

Indeed, even in today's hyper-connected world what most employers look for is not just technical expertise, but soft skills, especially when it comes to management and leadership roles.

Therefore even if you have an attained a bachelor's in a major, it will not suffice. Third, People with higher EQ tend to lean towards the entrepreneur field, as they are more eager to exploit opportunities, take risks, and turn creative ideas into actual innovations. (Well this book is undoubtedly part of this risk) All this makes EQ an outstanding quality to adapting to uncertain, unpredictable and complex environments.

CQ, on the other hand, stands for curiosity quotient. Author and journalist Thomas L. Friedman coined the following term to explain how curiosity can fuel the motivation of a person. Individuals with higher CQ are more inquisitive and open to new experiences. They find the unusual exciting and are quickly bored with routine. They tend to generate many original ideas and are counter-conformist. Studies with CQ are less intense as compared to EQ and IQ, but there's some evidence to suggest it is just as vital when it comes to managing complexity in two significant ways.

First, individuals with higher CQ usually have a liberal attitude towards other's interpretation and opinions. This distinct, mature, delicate thinking style defines the very core of complexity. Second, CQ leads to higher levels of intellectual investment and knowledge gain over a period, especially in formal domains of education, such as science and art. Knowledge and expertise, much like experience, translate complex situations into familiar ones, so CQ is the ultimate tool to produce simple solutions for complex problems.

Oh and allow me to quote the great Albert Einstein who mentioned that he have no special talent but was plain curious. This clearly is a hint there is a hidden genius in each one of us, really. How as the educators are we going to spark their sense of curiosity if they are constantly going through an endless routine based system?

I could clearly remember my final schooling years of just only scraping through life. The endless cycle of going to school, barely having my meals, rushing for tuition classes and struggling to complete assignments late at night was consuming my time.

When I mention tuition classes, it was the only way I could barely pass my examinations. The price was hefty. My father had to spend thousands of dollars to hire a tutor to teach me what is already in the textbook. I mean it sounds silly to have someone to tell me to read the textbook but I blindly still did it.

I thought I was doing myself a favour. I had to make my parents proud. If only I had knowledge on investing back then, I would have asked my dad to fund for my investment plans instead. That way even if I had not been successful, I could always try again as investing is one of the smartest ways to grow money.

It then brings us to the next gap in the system. The education system often misses the element of finance. Financial education is so essential to life. Many of us grow up to end up in debts and end up in a lot financial burden. Financial education is just as or even more important to learn than regurgitating facts and details of history on an exam paper. I never knew much about finance until I read the book Rich Dad, Poor Dad. The book primarily talks about financial independence. The simple language presenting in the book makes it easy to understand for teenagers. The main reason I brought this book up is how it has changed my perspective of money. Many including me believe that money is the root of all evil. However, this book begs to defer. I understand now that money is just a means, and it must not be the end goal. Hence there is a need for students to acquire financial knowledge in schools. In the future, it could save so many families and marriages as money is a reason why families split and marriages end.

I believe these gaps have existed so profoundly due to the notion of social conditioning. It is where we adopt everything in life basing on social conditioning. Education, media, elders, traditions are all part of the spectrum that teaches and helps our path in life. I had placed education first as that is what this whole book covers. However, by exploring the different influences of social conditioning, we can create a system that helps one flourish.

For instance, we have been socially conditioned only to see blood relatives as family and to think that dogs and kittens make the best of pets and not a cow or a tiger. In fact, the way we just view the above is not necessarily the truth. Even take fashion, masculinity, and feminism where society scripts the female and male roles that are represented by the current roles they play. It does not again have to be the truth.

When we talk about having to create a better education system, we need to come to the realisation that it is not just about syllabus and classroom set up which needs to be amended, you see both of that is only just a social conditioning from the previous generation which we have followed. It may be the very reason as to why many of you readers may become skeptical with bothering to considering the possibilities. You see just because everybody makes the mistake, it does not entitle it to be normal. People may make frequent remarks of how 'you cannot change everybody' and 'everybody is different'.

On the flip side, I refuse to believe of all this as all the sayings that I just mentioned is the result of social conditioning, it is all built on societal expectation. The society we live in, the culture we live in, the experiences we have, the upbringing we have and how things are classified as.

For instance, the average salary in Singapore could be entirely different in the United States of America and even in the United Kingdom. What is different in India for instance not eating pigs may be a perfectly normal behavior in China. We cannot just seal the deal by concluding that genetic material determines his or her behavior. Characteristics like selfishness and greed are not innate. I believe that we are all creatures of love, capable of being of compassionate.

If we can rise above social conditioning, we are then able to discover new possibilities. Social conditioning often set people up for the path of conformity and mediocrity. It can be a disaster if you are trying to elevate the standards of the education system. I believe it will be the biggest challenge but not impossible to achieve.

Good news is that these gaps and difficulties are not prevalent in all societies. I have to give credit to those who are more humanistic in the way they perceive education. The Germans are brilliant in the way they have crafted the system. Waldorf education is a prime example of how the education system could be. Rudolf Steiner, the founder of the Waldorf education, built a system following a holistic approach, where he took into the scientific account of the spirit, body, and soul connection and created a framework whereby the capacities of the above can unravel through the different developmental stages in an individual's life.

The students in this curriculum do not just read and write about subjects such as music, dance, literature, and theater theoretically but exposed to experience which helps stimulate them emotionally, physically and spiritually as well. Teachers assess them through personal development, and standardized tests are deficient in their system. There are currently 1000 Waldorf schools in 60 countries that show that change is possible.

Chapter 2

Empowering The Mind

The primary concern in schools these days will be the lack of skills to empower the minds of students. Teachers regularly ditch students to a state of how they are not good enough or that they have got to fight all the competition surrounding them. However, philosophers all believe that there are equal successes for each one of us. Moreover that it is our birthright that we can achieve anything we set our minds towards.

I will not deny the fact that there are great teachers and lecturers out there. Many motivate us to do better. However merely telling one to do better seems inadequate. Teachers must start inspiring the mind of the students and not only teach what is in the textbooks. Let us go back further in time to when we were a young baby. We will realise that no one taught us how to walk because we have the capability to do so ourselves. All we needed was someone to help us get back up when we fall. We can take that to practice by discarding the overfeeding of information to the minds of students. Instead, teachers can be more of a guide for students and instill independent learning.

It might then help students cope when they graduate, as they do not need much of it to survive in the real world. The independent learning then actually helps them navigate through the issues they may face on a daily basis.

I could recall a time when I had the opportunity to job shadow for Barclays. The risk team greeted us all. They went on to present their introductory speeches. The common words that were passed out were how microscopic of what we are doing in college is going to help us meet real job demands. I was taken aback when I heard it. Why then are we students led to struggle for years trying to obtain higher qualifications if ninety percent of it is going to be redundant? You might think I am exaggerating. Well, throwing such words in the mind of young people cannot bring something positive to the table. I was not only disappointed, but I could not comprehend how we still follow blindly to chase after the same qualifications.

Schools need to shift from merely instilling fear upon students to guiding them to what is essential for life and how we can receive results that will mean something. I say to discard instilling fear in the name of rigor and accountability. I can say this with experiences from my time in an institution where we were continually shown statistics on the rate of retaining students and had to hear lectures on how we need to push ourselves further. Simply saying work harder and push further only sounds vague than the answers a student scripts for her essay question. I mean what better will the students know if they are just loaded with redundant information and not sufficient guidance as to how to process the information. More so the concept of competition seems to be a trend these days where one force themselves to go through an education that they feel passionless about, only to end up in mediocrity.

I believe we can build a system that could brighten the future of students if we discard conformity. The problem is that we are constrained to limited beliefs and thinking. In fact, it is accepted as a norm. We are taught to be realists and to fit ourselves in a box. Great things occur outside a box. The educators must impress that upon our students from the very beginning, not to merely tell them to study subjects so that they can get a mediocre job. We need to educate the system to change the current definition and empower students to dream big. There is nothing logical and realistic about Steve Jobs or Mark Zuckerberg. What if we allow more of our students to find their own niche, imagine the possibilities that it could manifest?

It could give rise to innovations that could save our planet. Just by providing them knowledge about global warming in an air-conditioned classroom is not going to equip students to deal with the issue once they graduate from school. They are going to simply follow the herd and be ignorant about it. We are living in an existence where there is a loud call for action. Simply having good intentions is not going to suffice. We are already seeing the damage our earth is going through. Climate change is one. War, Poverty and lack of shelter are still very prevalent in this world. Such topics are only often conversed about on the surface level and are let to the big leaders to deal with. The fact that you are a human being is enough for you to act upon it. This has to be reinforced among the youth.

I have traveled around the globe to different continents and I have seen poverty, the refugees stranded in train stations and even hear stories from those who have run away from their countries that are in the war. It is hard for me to keep silent and ignore the problems in the world. The worst feeling is to encounter it and not be able to do anything about it. I then started reflecting on how my education in college is limited and it frustrates me that I lack in ways to give. How then do we as a whole get to the root of the matter? We need the right education to deal and tackle these issues. We need a system where we can create leaders who will look into all these problems and bring about change. I am embarrassed to say that we are creating more vicious people who are more fearful of their income status than the children who are dying out of starvation. Sure, there are a number of people bringing about change. I have seen and heard of some incredible human beings myself who are doing great work to make this world a better place. My question is about the majority. I believe group goals and collaborating is the most efficient way to establish solutions.

What if students were introduced to the fundamental laws of the universe and how everyone has a purpose to fulfill in this lifetime that also guarantees adequate success for each one of us in this planet? How marvelous will it be if teachers could empower each student by saying that each one of them literally matters as long as they take up space on earth and that all they got to actually find is their purpose in life which is to make this world we share a better place to live in.

I believe love is our true self and by instilling fear, it only reflects poorly on how our adults are handling the situation. After all, I do not genuinely blame anyone in the system for they might not know better themselves. However, thankfully due to the advancement in technology, it makes the learning for youths from the current millennia so much faster. That has indeed helped me and others understand more on the laws of the universe and less on competition. Books such as the 'secret' have introduced many to the law of attraction. This can help one understand that life does not run on autopilot. We indeed have full control to design our lives to our desire.

Schools could start aligning syllabus that will be tailored to meet the needs of students to avoid conformity. More so to meet the real need that they will require once they graduate. While writing this I saw a tweet "*too overwhelmed with school work to the extent I don't feel like talking to anyone at all*". This did not even surprise me as more and more students are isolating themselves due to pressure. Most of us subside to succumb to isolation. The easiest way to reduce this negative behavior is if they could start questioning the things they do. The issues that could empower students to feel socially connected. This, as a result, will make them look forward to building humanity.

Then the question is why are schools and colleges not empowering students to ask the right type of questions to achieve their desires? Vishen Lakhiani, CEO of Mind Valley published an article titled '3 most important questions' and the questions were "*What experiences and objects do you seek to have in life*? "*How do you see yourself grow*?" and "*How would you contribute to the betterment of the planet*?" When I first read it, I thought how brilliant will it be if teachers ask these questions to their students. I believe it will positively affect the perspective students have towards goal setting. It will also serve as a powerful motivation for students to perform better.

To merely follow what society think is ideal can be damaging to youths these days. It is no surprise that more and more youth's fall under depression, social anxiety, and low self-esteem. We cannot just let these issues pass for they are important triggers caused by the body to signal that something is really wrong. We can easily blame it on the background of the student. The circumstances, for instance, the environment that the child was brought up. The irony is that students spend so many hours in school in a week. More than the quality time they get to spend with their family and friends. Hence how is it that institutions are never once to be blamed? This may simply be the stereotype that schools only serve them well.

However does it really?

My suggestion will be to not invest so much time in parents teacher meet. This honestly seems to serve little purpose. The teacher or parents cannot always claim that they understand the turmoil the student goes through. The teachers or parents may feel that they have surpassed the age of adolescence. This may allow them to think that they are capable of understanding the behavior of the student.

However psychologically one can never be able to understand the degree of pain or emotion that another is going through. Therefore I am not offending anybody or victimizing the students in any case. My hope is to seek a transformation in the education system that could truly help an individual liberate in life.

Most students seek much of their reliance upon external circumstances for acceptance. This then pushes them into a conforming condition that does barely anything to elevate education or personal growth. Institutions must educate students that material things and outer traits will not sustain them long term. Schools must also instill in them that growth comes from contribution and from cultivating inner qualities. Female students spend so much of their time in agony to look cute and Male students much of their time to look sturdy and built.

This is not just a gender issue. It is silently enforced within the parameters of the schools and colleges. In school you have students joining different cliques, you have the favorite misses, sharp looking misters, the weird ones, the nerdy others and the list goes on if you have been to school.

Most of them feel the need to be the cream of the crop of the list. They spend so much time and effort in trying to do so. This, in the long run, does not matter at all and it takes an awful journey to understand so. I feel empathy towards students who gets involved in relationships and courses only because it looks attractive on the outside. I have been there myself. Some are even proud to call them shallow minded. This just brings for some serious look into the system that these people go through. This then reinforces the fact the system is spiritually weak. An individual who is spiritually fed will only ever uplift another so the system definitely needs a spiritual boost.

When I was younger I use to feel like the character, blossom, on the series of power-puff girls, a television show of my childhood times. Blossom was the one with the most power and she was strong as well. However as I slowly began to grow up with the influence of teachers and society, all I did was follow. Follow what the crowd did, follow how the group spoke and to be honest it made me develop an inferiority complex as I was trying to fit standards that never made sense. The characteristics of the character blossom in me slowly diminished.

The confidence and strength I had when I was a child seemed to almost disappear as I was journeying through this self-destructing system. I was putting myself through self-hate and anxiety. I had petite confidence and let alone a voice to share my opinions. I was a bubbly girl by nature but all of it started waning due to my esteem issues. Little did I know back then, that it was all a delusional chatter that was being entertained by my subconscious mind that was programmed to conformity? I was trying to fit standards of the society that initially purses hypocrisy. We all go through esteem issues at one point or another. It may even be blamed on the individual but what better will the individual know on how to manage his or her mental and emotional self if they are not provided the right education.

Yes, I agree that there are counselors, psychologists, and psychiatrists to help people with mental health. However, not everyone wants to come to terms with his or her issues and willing find these professional for a solution.

This is why it is necessary that schools provide them with the basics of spirituality. This will be essential for students to understand themselves on a deeper level. They will able to identify what triggers their self-esteem issues and even try to combat it with some of the spirituality tools.

Educators can also look into alternatives to building a new curriculum that can include hypnosis that could target subconscious mind as a reconditioning process to see abundance in the world we live in today. Hypnosis may sound negative. We need a system that follows the framework along the lines of personal growth. This could include creative visualization. These tools could help them attain a holographic feeling that they are already a success. This is also empowering to students. Imagine what this could do if it was routinized instead of reading mundane textbooks that often put students to a deep slumber.

Creative visualization

I consider myself still a student of the subject. I try to practice and often times when I do it works. I have used it to successfully get through interviews and many a times it has saved me from a great deal of trouble. One instance will be during my recent trip to Rome, Italy. I had discovered all of the beauty there and was trying to head to Athens, Greece to catch my flight back home. Athens is pronounced athina in Europe. (Take note of this) I booked a train ticket to athina and I ended up in the countryside of Italy. The place seemed deserted and I felt so lost. I honestly could not believe what was happening. Everyone there could not speak English. They were speaking to me in Italian to understand how I ended up there. Although I felt terrible, I just kept visualizing myself getting out of the situation.

By this time I was trying to show my tickets and tell them I was supposed to go to Athens in Greece. Also at this point everyone in that country had surrounded me. I was literally the talk of the town. A friendly old man then approached me and showed me his Google translate app in his phone. I thanked all the technology gods in the world and started slowing making conversations (by typing on his app) with him trying to explain my situation. After an hour or so they finally figured that I came to the wrong place and that there is a place called athina in Italy itself. They then called a woman down and she could speak a couple of English words. She told me that the only way I could get back to Greece is from Rome and that I could only take a flight. I felt a little relieved but I was unsure of how to get to Rome. The man who helped me earlier offered to give me a ride to his slaughterhouse and that someone there could help me book a ticket and bring me to the terminal to get a bus back to Rome. It sounded bizarre that I had to go a slaughterhouse especially so that I was vegan. However I was left with no choice and I just kept visualizing and followed him. His family was there and I felt relieved. His daughter helped me booked the tickets and his son took me to dinner and gave me a ride to the terminal and I safely arrived in Rome the next day. I could have easily ended up in a lot of trouble. Creative visualization really helped me that day to avoid it all.

What exactly is creative visualization?

The wise Albert Einstein understood that "Your imagination is your preview of lives coming attractions." Creative visualization acts as the catalyst for the chosen attractions.

Creative visualization is the art of using imagination to manifest your desired life. It is a form of imagery therapy. In fact, it is not something unusual. You might already be using it on a daily basis. Imagination is innate in us. It is considered to be the basic creative energy of the universe. We might not be aware of it as many of us use it in an unconscious way. Creative visualization can act as a simple tool to reprogram the subconscious mind.

Imagination is the skill to create an idea, a mental image, and impressions in the mind. When we focus on the idea and give it positive energy, it manifests itself. It makes it easy to attain goals in all aspects of life. Say you want to manifest good grades or get fit or buy a new home. You can imagine yourself into achieving it. It can work for both positive and negative situations. By focusing on what you desire and feeling the emotions even before you have reached it, it makes it easier for you to be in the frequency of manifesting it. Give it more details and imagery and it becomes faster for you to attain it. You do not have to be even spiritual to use this technique. You just have to be open to the ideas and see what happens for you and you can develop it further with when you see the changes.

Creative visualization does not just help you achieve goals. It can help you gain better health, as your emotions will be more intact. It makes you more confident and also allows you to forge meaningful relationships. Lastly, it helps you break free from stress. Legends like Oprah, Bill Gates, and Will Smith have used and vouched for creative visualization as a technique that works.

Quantum physics also agrees with the process of creative visualisation, and it states that by thinking thoughts of a particular outlook when visualizing, we will probably attract the experience energetically. It is so as we know from Quantum Physics that everything is energy. That includes our thoughts. When we combine this with the law of attraction, it is easier to understand the way it works.

Creative visualization also works best paired with a few factors. States of mind is essential when we want visualization to become more effective. States of mind include, Alpha, Beta, Theta, Delta and Gamma. When we are conscious, our mind is usually in the state of Beta. However for creative visualization, it is better for us to be in the Alpha state. It is the state of mind that we are in when we wake up or when we feel sleepy. This is so as it is easier to get into a meditative feel when we are in the above scenarios.

Creative visualisation also works best paired with a few factors. States of mind are essential when we want visualization to become more efficient. States of mind include Alpha, Beta, Theta, Delta, and Gamma. When we are conscious, our mind is usually in the state of Beta. However, for creative visualization, it is better for us to be in the Alpha state. It is the state of mind that we are in when we wake up or when we feel sleepy. It is so as it is easier to get into a meditative feel when we are in the above scenarios.

Mental health has become a controversial topic in the education system present. Especially after joining a university, students are more anxious and are likely to develop depression. It is not surprising to hear that the environment in a university can be stressful and daunting. If you only Google for statistics on the rates of mental health among students, you will find yourself scrolling through pages of data. The statistics are really disturbing to hear.

I believe that schools must then take responsibility in working towards nurturing an individual holistically. This will help students become mentally stronger and live a robust life. This also helps enable them to quickly take on challenges in the future.

Chapter 3
Mindfulness

The practice of mindfulness is to engage in the moment-to-moment awareness of body sensations and feelings. I believe it is an ancient art that is very much needed in our modern lives. Mindfulness is often prescribed in therapy and studied about in psychology. Mindfulness is to look at things more objectively and it is fundamental that it reaches the masses in schools. I emphasize that schools must adopt mindfulness as a valuable skill as I could only imagine how well I could have handled situations in life if I were taught about it in school. I had to reach my tipping point in order to be aware of practices like mindfulness.

Mindfulness also has the power to harness kindness in a being. Kindness, a concept that may sound simple can be foreign in schools. Key issues in schools including bullying could be eradicated if such skills are cultivated among students. In fact, there will be a boost in each student's self-esteem and compassion.

I will not deny that schools do not invest in such curriculum but doing so for an hour a week at most seems insufficient. Back in my school days, I had this curriculum called civics moral education where we were taught different values that come with a story and a reflection activity for the student to do each week. This activity lasted for less than an hour a week.

What is worse is that it is one of the lessons where no one tends to pay any attention. I vividly remember how my classmates and I will either fall asleep or even better try to complete our unfinished assignments. It is hard to blame as what good would it do them if there were not enough emphasis placed on life morals but merely on completing more essays on history and homework on math equations.

In this new era, everyone has an access to a smartphone. It is even more important for mindfulness. If we do not learn to take control of ourselves, the gadgets we use will do the job for us. We need a system to teach us to notice the present moment. We need to learn to understand it and be grateful for it.

We can learn to incorporate simple mindfulness practices in our daily lives. One way is by allowing yourself to count breaths when you want to become aware of how rapid or shallow your breathing is. You can also focus on long inhalations and exhalations that help with the process.

You can also try closing your eyes in random surroundings to feel a state of panic or learn to greet the objects and nature around you. All of these simple practices could do you so much good as it helps rectify that you are a conscious mindful person. (I assure you will not become a hippie after this)

If you sense that your muscles are tightening or say that you have pins and needles. You can stop to be aware of your body and recognize how your energy is flowing in your body.
Most usually ignore it but you could take it as a moment to be mindful. These are some mindfulness practices that I have learned in my journey to personal growth.

Lakhotia, S. (2012), state that it is important to *'understand that the physical world is just a mirror of deeper intelligence. Intelligence is the invisible organiser of all matter and energy, and since a portion of this intelligence resides in you, you share in the organising power in the cosmos."* This is then proof that we are all connected and that we must all play our part to save humanity and the earth. What good can we offer if we are not adequate? Hence it is why we must be spiritually well to be able to see the bigger picture and live with purpose.

We got to realize that we are all in this together and be more mindful. Thus the desperate need for mindfulness in our daily lives including at school, work, and home.

I believe meditation is going to be the next big revolution in helping raise human potential. It is also the lifeline that we are all in need of given the circumstances. Meditation is the practice in which one is able to get a better grip on their mind. It enables one to gain better mental health and clarity.

Meditation allows one to be better aware of their breathing and it also helps one to relax. Apart from the calming benefits, it helps a being to tap into their inner guidance system that can help one discover the true purpose of why they are placed on earth. It truly is a powerful practice as it helps one relieve anxiety, fear and all that ugly feelings that causes one to feel inferior. Furthermore, when one is able to meditate effectively, he or she is able to connect to their highest power. This could include a boost in one's creativity or even able one to think more sharply.

Most of us are so willing to take good care of ourselves physically, by buying the best toiletries and that is a great thing. However, most of us never take the time to clean up the mess and dirt that is running through our minds always. Meditation in one way is the cleaning tool to empty the trash in our mind. It can help one to perceive problems as opportunities. It helps one feel refreshed and energized. In addition, it puts us in a state of bliss. I believe happiness and love are what we all crave for. We have to realise that it all comes from within.

Meditation has been the practice since the early eastern days to guide one in achieving all that there is and more. Many of you might be mocking me by asking if I'm trying to hire monks in schools and that is definitely not what I am pledging for. There are many myths about meditation that we have to first debunk.

Firstly, meditation is not just a scene of one sitting in a cross-legged position or what the Buddhist calls a lotus position with their palms facing upwards with the tips of the thumb and fingers gently touching each other.

Sure it is a way but various kinds of meditation can be way more practical and be part of the curriculum. Before I move further with what will work in a school environment, let us take a look at the five essential kinds of meditation. I learned this briefly when I went for talks on transcendental meditation.

Firstly we have the concentration meditation, of which I would say the regular kind. It is similar to the lotus position meditation where you will require effort, and it is not natural. It requires you to concentration on an object. It could be a flaming candle, the waves of the sea or a gemstone. It is the result of directed thought. The directed thought acts as a force. The more it develops, the more it can retain some of the concentration that can assist with liberation. It happens as when you focus on that one particular object, negative emotions such as greed, hate, jealousy may disappear.

Secondly, we have the contemplation where meaning is involved, and there is a local value. Contemplation is slightly different to concentration. It is a state of mind where there is a control of thoughts but at the same time it is left open to receive. If you were to concentrate on a zebra, you would examine the zebra very thoroughly. You may even count the stripes, of which is black and white and so on.

If you were to contemplate on the same zebra, you would leave your mind open to learning something about its environment, its physical function, its mental function and so on.

The conscious mind is rather like a monkey. Immediately we sit down to concentrate on something in silence, our mind climbs onto different branches and not staying still. If this happens to you, do not think for a moment that you are odd, or that you are a monkey brain. It happens to everyone who attempts it for the first time. You can get over it.

Lastly, we have the diving meditation that includes transcendental meditation, kundalini yoga whereby you dive within yourself. A little back-story with my experience before I go on to explain. I was in Budapest, Hungary on a summer afternoon with my friends. We were walking the beautiful streets where people were performing. As we got closer to see the performance, I saw white European women wearing sarees (an Indian traditional costume) and singing "*Hare Krsna, Hare Krsna, Krsna Krsna, Hare Hare, Hare Rama Hare Rama, Rama Rama, Hare Hare.*" We were fascinated, and when we asked them what was going on, they just held our hands, and they told us to follow along. We then started chanting the mantra, and we followed the way they were dancing so gracefully. It was moments of joy and laughter. We were grinning widely. It was a glimpse of bliss as we had completely immersed ourselves in it without thinking about anything else. After a while we got tired, and we left. We then went on to explore the other streets.

We were also still talking about how happy that just made us feel. Just as we were conversing, another European lady in a saree approached me and handed a book. I accepted it out of curiosity. The book was titled Chant and be Happy.

It was a book on the power of mantra meditation. What a coincidence I thought. My mind was trying to grasp what had just happened, and here a lady wanted to help me understand by handing me a book. I was just taken aback by awe. I went on to read it, and here I will discuss what I have learned from it. The mind acts as the vehicle, and it often uses a sound or mantra. Mantra is a Sanskrit word. Man means "mind" and try means "to deliver". Thus it is a transcendental sound vibration that has the potential to liberate the mind from any means of conditioning. The mantra usually sets a wave to accommodate the technique. The "*Hare Krsna*" mantra that I mentioned is one of the many mantras that one can use. While reading the book, I got to know that famous singer and songwriter John Lennon was practicing mantra meditation when he was part of the Beatles. I am giving this example to show that it is practical to use, and it is not limited to the hippies. Not to mention, the Beatles were one of the most successful bands in history.

In the primary stages of chanting, practitioners can experience a clearer consciousness, peace of mind and even resist bad temptations. By developing a realisation, they can perceive a spiritual existence of their self.

Practicing mantra meditation initially focuses on controlling the mind. This power comes from being caged to our usual thoughts and desires. These thoughts and desires are usually materialistic, and it wants the mind to achieve it to experience the matter.

It constantly is restless and attempts to seek more pleasure. In Buddhism, this is the very reason is the cause of suffering. We are very often holding on to attachments, and there is always an undercurrent of yearning in life. Take, for instance; you buy a car that is brand X. Maybe brand Y is better. Since your finance only allows you to purchase brand X. You are guaranteed to have a yearning for brand Y still while buying brand X. As such the carnal mind always tries to seek pleasure by expecting the senses to experience materialistic things and relationships. It makes one always to be unsatisfactory with life. It also means that it is harder to achieve peace. Thus chanting a mantra can act as a form of control over the mind.

How can a mantra do that? Srila Prabhupada explains, "Our entanglement in material affairs has begun from a material sound." He also points out, "There is sound in the spiritual world also. If we approach that sound, then our spiritual life begins." From this, we can understand that by approaching the sound in the spiritual world we can tame our restless mind that keeps yearning for more.

Mantra meditation can also help to gain knowledge of self. In Buddhism, it is necessary that we must not get attached to our existence. It may sound a little absurd. However, if we are open to it, we can understand that our physical being is often an illusion. When the living being is too keen with the material body, it can lose track of its spiritual existence. He or she then is inevitably fearful of disease, death, and aging.

It could cause multiple anxieties on different occasions. The practice of mantra meditation can realign your consciousness back to the original state. In this state, you can gain more awareness of your authentic self that does not include your physical being. We no longer have to be caged behind our false identities like for instance, "I am Asian" or I am European" We just become one with the universe. It is what true liberation is.

These are the gist of the types of meditation as more are covered in detail in books that I will share at the end. There is another misconception of meditation. It is how it could stop thoughts from entering your mind and that it may even silence your mind. I am here to tell you no. It is not a practice where you smile and say 'Namaste'. It does not work that way.

Meditation is not just a dip in the Jacuzzi pool like how many have promoted it to be. If you were to ask an authentic meditator, he or she would tell you that it brings up more physiological content revolving around past hurts and traumas. It is only by facing your darkness that you can step into the light, which is the real idea behind meditation.

Hence there is a pressing need for mindfulness practices like meditation to be imparted in the adolescence. One major advantage of meditation is that it helps in the strengthening of the prefrontal cortex.

An article edited by Edward E. Smith states "in addition, changes in electroencephalogram and cortical thickness have been reported in long-term meditation practitioners of compassion and insight meditation." From this we can understand that by strengthening the prefrontal cortex intelligence in a being is likely to increase.

Willoughby Britton, a researcher at Brown University, mentions jokingly how the "*adolescence is classified as the clinical population*". It is so as the prefrontal cortex is the weakest at this age. It is why our dear teenagers are more prone to disorders like depression and anxiety. According to the University of Rochester Medical Centre, our prefrontal cortex does not reach full development until the age of twenty-five. Hence it is vital that educators work towards strengthening the prefrontal cortex. Educators do not have to make students sit for a forty minute long meditation, just actions that could allow the natural evolution to take place.

A remedy could include dispensing unregulated time in the academic curriculum. It must not include recess or lunch break. It must be a time for students to reconnect to the sense of being in their minds. This leeway of time and space will help attune them back to the present moment. Creativity and innovation also spark in the flow of mind and pockets of time.

The whole idea of this is to cut some slack from the operant conditioning process that is taking place. You see when students are in their classes listening to lessons. They are mentally preparing themselves for a future moment. It is as simple as a student thinking that he must pay attention to class so that he will not fail his exams. This conditioning known as operant conditioning is hindering his natural state of being. Giving students the privilege of unstructured time in school could greatly benefit their awareness. When presented with something new, the awareness they have gained could easily allow them to grasp it.

We need to understand that schools can easily teach mindfulness can be easily in school and to prove this we have projects such as 'mindful' schools in the United States where schools offer courses for learning mindfulness. I believe more nations could adopt a similar approach. With mindfulness, one will be able to respond in a wiser manner that could result in longer periods of attention span, learning, emotional resilience, understanding and conflict settlement.

With mindfulness making a scene in the classroom, students will learn how to respond as to react. Often times, students tend to act and it usually shadows a defensive nature. Thus it is necessary that students get to respond which shadows a more thoughtful nature.

Psychology shows how without mindfulness the stimulus naturally tends to react and with it, they learn to respond as mindfulness acts as a bridge for a flow to occur in the space between the desired response and stimulus.

Mindfulness techniques could also help adolescents diagnosed with ADHD. Chris McKenna gave a talk at Google on mindfulness neurobiology and children where he suggests how tapping ourselves physically could be a solution. It helps in the development of children as it could assist in determining physical boundaries such as finding the limbs, which is crucial. Institutions must introduce such techniques instead of punishment and negative reinforcement to students for being disruptive in school.

Another method and probably a solution that the educators could consider is the emotional freedom technique, which is also known as the tapping solution. Nick Ortner, is the author of the book the tapping solution, is the founder of the tapping world Summit and best-selling filmmaker of the tapping solution.

He wrote a book about the tapping solution and how it is one of the easiest and fastest ways to address both emotional and physical problems that tend to hinge our lives. The tapping solution is a physical tapping on the energy meridians of the body while focusing on the current issue and by verbalizing statements.

The tapping is proven to help calm the nervous system and bring back the balance in the energy of the body. This kind of conditioning could rethread the brain and eliminate negative patterns that keep an individual stuck.

A tapping solution is a practical tool and there is science to substantiate. Educators need to adopt this to instill in students who go through stress on a regular basis. The problem in a school environment is that everyone claims that they are stressed.

The word stress has become a buzzword. It is all fair as students are going through the pressure of having to clear assignments and ace their examinations. However what we lack to realise is the current depth of this stress and how one lives daily being ignorant about how it permeates through their entire body. The tapping solution works because when you are tapping on the meridian points, you are sending signals to the amygdala.

The amygdala is the fight or flight response that gets triggered when faced with danger. Say, for instance, a tiger in a jungle is chasing you. Then it is necessary that the amygdala switch gets turned on since there is not a lot of thinking to do when you have a tiger chasing you.

It means that ideally the switch in the amygdala must be turned off. However, we are living a routinized life where we are not even aware of how much stress our bodies are piling on. We are chronically abusing the switch of the amygdala, which then causes us to deal with phobias, panic attacks, anxiety disorder, and addictions.

Students who suffer from this do realise that they must not act this way. However, they are unable to do so due to the programming of their subconscious mind. When the amygdala response is taking place, most of the oxygen is being sent down to the arms and legs to prepare us for flight, fight or freeze. It results in lesser oxygen for our cognitive abilities or prefrontal cortex making it tough for us to think actually. It is why stress is bad, and how one thinks it could motivate us to accomplish more is false. That is why there is a crucial need for techniques such as the tapping solution to come into play in a school or university. This simple technique of tapping could ultimately help lower levels of cortisol and build more self-confidence and boost health in general for them to perform more efficiently in the school environment.

Chapter 4

The concept of happiness

Happiness is the natural state of being and positivity is the growth state. Neuroscience now tells us that happy, active people live much longer than others. There are new studies that show the importance of capitalizing on the happiness advantage. Shawn Anchor wrote the 'Happiness Advantage'. It became a hit with many that he managed to give one of the most popular TED talk titled "The happy secret to better work.' I think educators can learn one or two things from him as he mentioned that his ideas could work in any setting. The gist of his talk is telling his audience that they have to be happy to become successful in all aspects of life. Most of us are prone to think that hard work comes first, and Happiness is often the result. Our parents, teachers all tell us to work hard to be successful and eventually happy.

However, in his book, he goes to show with years of research on the topic of happiness, that it is, in fact, the opposite that is true. Through his study and stay at Harvard and his many travels, he has gathered data to prove that indeed when you put happiness first, you succeed better at whatever that you have set out to pursue.

Happiness is not a result of something. I believe happiness is much like math. It requires practice. Sometimes you got to practice it daily to achieve it. It then has to be discussed with students to allow them a peace of mind.

Students then will not wonder why they end up not as happy as students thought they would be when they finally achieve their goals. For instance, receiving a scholarship and still not feeling as satisfied.

Here are some suggestions on happiness can be taught at school. Firstly will be the spirituality practice of meditation. We have discussed on meditation in the earlier topic so I will not ramble on. Neurologists have proven time and time again on how meditation can alter your brain functions. Meditation is accessible through countless apps.

Secondly will be to encourage the act of anticipation among students. *"The pleasure isn't in doing the thing, the pleasure is in planning it."* It was a quote mentioned by the author, John Green. It is indeed the anticipation of something that gets us all excited. It is good news as it means that even if a student is not sure how well he or she is going to perform. Just thinking about a positive result can increase levels of endorphins. It is not just wishful thinking. It is more of a creative visualisation process that I have discussed in the earlier chapters.

Third will be gratitude. I have read so many books on personal growth, and all of it covers gratitude in one way or another. Gratitude is simply genius. Most of us complain about what we do not have and often live in our little misery bubbles. Those who are grateful however live in the magic of abundance.

Why? Well, when you are thankful you look for the right and naturally better comes to you. It is a law of attraction. What you seek, seeks you. Students can be told to write a gratitude list at any time they like in a day. It will train them always to see the good in things and become happier in the long term.

Fourthly will be to infuse positivity in our environment. I believe environment plays a significant role in happiness. Marie Kondo talks about how tidying up can be life changing that she wrote a book about it. Marie Kondo mentions in her book "Tidying is a special event. Don't do it every day". I think that is brilliant as students and teachers can come up with a unique roster to tidy their classrooms. I do know that this already in practice in most schools. In fact, it was a practice in all the schools I have enrolled. However, no one is ever excited. Most see it as a burden. Many might even think that it is the job of the cleaners to do it. I advocated for the change in the way of thinking. If students could see tidying as an art to change their lives, they may take it more seriously and yet have fun at the same time. Teachers and students can even come together to discuss ways they can fabricate their classrooms. It will make the environment a happier place to thrive for both the teacher and students.

Fifth will be to educate students about money. Money is not the root of all evil. It is how you spend it that determines your quality of life and character. The book, 'The Happiness Advantage" explains how when research shows that those who spend money on experiences with their loved ones happened to feel happier than those who spend money on shoes, bag, and accessories. Also, those who spend money on others almost often feel more satisfied at the end of the day. My takeaway from the book is how essential it is less materialistic. It is a message that rarely gets out to the mainstream. Most people tend to spend fortunes on a material, and this is something that we must not encourage to students.

Media encourages not just students but to the general public to buy things that are not even necessary. Hence it is vital that schools also alongside their parents help in raising students to learn to spend their money wisely. Sure, it is nice to buy a material once in a while, but we must remind ourselves that they will not guarantee happiness.

Sixth will be to encourage students to do what they love truly. It is so essential to do what you love. I feel as we take on more responsibilities, we tend not to prioritise activities that make us sparkle. It could be traveling, craft, sport, language or even culinary practice. Exercising what you love to do is valuable to your sanity. It must be stressed to students as they are young and living in a bubble of comfort may hinder their full potential of expressing themselves.

Last but not least, to physically exercise. It is almost a no-brainer that exercising regularly helps us keep fit and healthy. You might have also heard that exercising regularly helps release endorphins that are pleasure inducing. It not only helps in boosting your mood but your performance at work or school. Sports are a curriculum in school. I am well aware of it. However, the curriculum could sometimes be rigid. For instance, you are only allowed to play a particular sport and students may not get to pick what they want to play. Hence introducing a variety could get students to look forward to exercising. My suggestion will be even to introduce mindfulness yoga, as it will be the perfect blend of mindfulness and body exercise.

Establishing some of the above in institutions could bring about great change. There will be no need for unnecessary practices such as detention and punishment. In return, such practices will in all ways contribute to higher productivity levels.

Happiness is what we all often crave. It will be so empowering for students to realize that they can relinquish the need for external approval to achieve it. They can then be able to judge their worth based on what they value. It is an excellent way to replace the fear-motivated behaviour with love-motivated behaviour. What comes out of love is usually beautiful.

I am not trying to sound poetic. There is data contributing to how only when a person is vibrating at a higher-level frequency would he or she can manifest any goals in life. Love is inevitably the highest form of energy. Christie Marie Sheldon, Founder of love or above states on her website that "500 is the vibration of love" and how "when you vibrate at this level life can become drastically different" She is indeed right.

We as Westerners are fond of our physical bodies. We follow rituals rooted in the physical world. We are taught to think in the physical world, to identify where the symptoms and problems lie in all aspects of our life. What we fail to realize is that we as a human being have a duality within us.

Dualists in the philosophy of mind mention that we have two bodies; one is our physical body, which is made up of matter that is composed of atoms. The other will be the energetic body.

We all know that everything that surrounds us is energy. The screen that you are looking at now to the plants outside your window to the waves that kiss the shore to the cup of tea that you are holding in your hand, it is all energy. Sounds like basic science. Well in fact it is. Since energy is what we are made of we, give out energy too. If that does not sound convincing, try rubbing the both of your palms vigorously.

Notice the energy pulsating out or do you feel a sort of pressure or even tingles? All of this could help you guide on what your current blocks are in life.

It is when you address your energy body that you will be able to see positive changes in your life. Instead of taking action in the physical world, we might consider having to heal our energy body first. Not the other way round. Working with energy is directly opposite to the physical work. Working with energy involves imagination, and there is no limit to what one could imagine whereas, in the physical world, there is only so much you can run after.

Say, if your relationships are not sailing smoothly, it could be because of a particular block of energy in your body. But what do we do? We go after the person, trying to set things right and end up in a bigger argument. Another great instance will be the adults who invariably instill in one that money does not come easy and that you got to work hard to be rich. Most of the younger generation is also indifferent about it. As a result, we just work ourselves to mental exhaustion feeling dissatisfied. It is only time that we evolve to seek out creative ways to live our dreams and activate our energy bodies. One can only vibrate at a higher frequency when he or she can feel emotions such as happiness and love and positive beliefs.

I would not have had a single clue about energy duality concept if I had been stuck in the system reading textbooks that equip me with less valuable information. We do not learn how to survive through hardships or pursue happiness by reading our textbooks.

We were programmed with love when we were born, regardless of our ethnicity or background. We had the tendency to love as it is innate. Why is that when we grow up all of that beauty is gone? It is because we have been taught to focus elsewhere, that we have been conditioned to think unnaturally, to think of competition, struggle, finite resources, scarcity and limitations that contradict who we are. We began to think them and know them as a result. However, love is the existential fact and the purpose of life. It is the ultimate reality of life. It is why we are all placed on this planet.

It sounds like proof to me that it is worth investing in the happiness levels of students in schools. It will be a positive ripple effect as energy affects those around you.

Chapter 5

Building strong relationships

Building healthy relationships is so essential for one to stay mentally stable. We live in an interconnectedness world where all of us in one form or another connect to each other. Therefore it is wise for institutions to ponder the vitality of strong relationships with students. Institutions do conduct the usual group and pair sharing that takes place during lessons. While such efforts are in place, we still see students who are anti-social and lonely.

Are we all not one? Bob Marley did not just sing the song one love for fun. It is the fundamental truth. What if everyone was able to forge great relationships with the prior knowledge that we live in a world where we are all connected in one way or another regardless of our background? We could all then realise the vitality of healthy relationships that can make us happy and build a more comfortable world with combined efforts.

Let us take a look at the business community. The one key factor bosses are looking for is communication and networking skills. In my free days, I got the opportunity to attend a few seminars. Most workshops talk about the importance of communication and how we need to learn how to network with others to grow our potential. I have to admit that I was always one of the younger participants in the seminars.

People who attended the workshops were dressed up smartly in their business attires. It made me realise that even those that looked favorable on the exterior has skills lacking that they had to be present there for the seminars. It then brings me back to my argument of why I feel that educators have to build a curriculum based on building strong relationships.

It is not just going to help an individual communicate, but it will contribute to reducing bigotry, prejudices, and stigmas that we hold towards others as we live in a more diverse culture than ever in the past due to globalization. From all of my experience, I have learned that the best way to build strong relationships is by allowing yourself to be vulnerable. The act of vulnerability appears to be negative. It is entirely justified, as you have to be tough to survive in most societies. However, with the wall that you put up, you diminish the value of the relationships that you could potentially forge.

I was a nervous wreck when I first arrived at Timisoara, Romania, for a volunteering project. I felt overwhelmed to meet a bunch of internationals and Romanians whom I have never met before. I thought it was going to be difficult to make friends or even become close to any of them. I am naturally an introverted person, and it takes me time to open up. The point is that it was terrifying to meet new people and having to live with international students made me want to hide.

I soon realise that I had to be vulnerable and let them see me for who I am. If I am not going to reveal myself deeply to anyone, I will never be able to establish healthy relationships.

Take your family for instead, the main reason why family usually takes more importance than friends is because they know you in a deeper sense. Thus I decided to wear my courage jacket and dive into the vulnerability pool. What happens after was amazing. The more I started talking and sharing, the more I felt accepted and cherished. All I had to come out of my shell and be vulnerable.

It may sound complicated, but when you connect with people in an authentic way, you make it easier for the other person to engage with you. It is because everyone goes through the feeling of fear and shame. You are not alone. Best believe that when you put yourself out there, you will be able to connect with another. I am so happy that I made the choice to be vulnerable during the trip. I have made friends that I will stay in contact for a lifetime even though they are miles apart.

In the very popular Ted Talk, the power of vulnerability, Dr. Brene Brown said so eloquently that if you numb vulnerability, you also numb the birthplace of joy, belonging and creativity. It is very true. You can never just avoid a bad feeling and accept a good feeling. All feelings have to be felt by the bones for it do its job.

Well, then how do you get started on allowing yourself to be vulnerable and building genuine relationships? I hear you. Dr. Brene Brown said in her book the power of vulnerability, like with all things, it takes practice, the practice of believing that you are worthy of joy and belonging, to only tell you "you are enough." These three words hold so much power than we can imagine. You can try by looking in the mirror each day and repeat "I am enough." I thought it seemed ridiculous when I heard Dr. Louise Hay mention that in one of her speeches. Well, at least that was my initial thought. Hence I decided to try it. I used to suffer from mild acne at the point and to say those simple words, "I am enough" each time I looked in the mirror was rather difficult. I do not even have to say how much the media has polluted the minds of youth to look polished like porcelain. I still decided to do so every day, and I can say that the healing journey began.

I started developing a deeper sense of self-love. I felt whole as a person that not only made me feel confident. It also made me want to interact more with others. Yes, in the beginning, you will not believe what you say. However, when you keep repeating it, your mind will start thinking it and commence your healing process. Every word and emotion hold a frequency and energy that could either elevate you or make you crumble. It is then wise to make sure your mental chatter is mostly positive.

Hence the essence of building healthy boils down to the relationship that you have with yourself. The communication, be it the language or content is secondary to the nature of building strong relationships.

Chapter 6

Art of communication

Communication is crucial to everything in life. Whether it to order food at a restaurant or to try, explain something to your spouse during a fight, effective communication is necessary. Institutions do often teach the importance of communication in theory. I remember taking a subject called management of business where a good portion dedicated to communication. However, like dance and drama, communication is an art form that has to be mastered to benefit one. It is where the system is lacking in the exposure given to students to communicate on a daily basis.

"Hush hush." I could not keep count of the number of times I have been asked to keep quiet in class even when there are instances where I genuinely would have a conversation about the lesson with a peer. In the end, I only have been asked to keep my mouth shut and be called upon to pay complete attention to the teacher even if I did not understand what she is uttering.

I have even written essays to explain and apologise for speaking in class during my secondary school days. If we all taught to do is to remain quiet. When are we going to master the use of our voice that is a natural gift to given to express our internal dialogue?

If a being has to be forced to suppress it, it is no surprise that teenagers end up having fear and anxiety as they are supposed to listen and be quiet all the time. It is not to say that listening does not matter. It is equally important to receive but not to the extent of the students having to lose their voice.

There is a study that says that only seven percentage of communication is through words. I had learned this while listening to a Tony Robbins speech. I feel that the importance of building rapport must be looked into and taught to our students to improve the way they connect with one another. Many students might think they are better off by themselves. At least that was my way of thinking when I was younger. My pathetic reason was my intolerance to engage in a conversation with another being. I was preoccupied with my technological devices. I mean what had happened to compassion that we all humans possess internally?

When will our inner light shine if one is not taught to go out of their boundaries and reach out to each other? Most of the seminars and talks that I attend physically or listen via audios all mention that these are skills and knowledge you will never be able to attain in school! What does that even mean?

Why do we even go to school if we know we are going to end up remaining an average person and worst still never to be able to grow into our truest potential and contribute back to the community?

To be educated is one who can make a change or difference, but most of the graduates have only sufficient time to complain about what they have and remain unhappy. What if institutions teach them to communicate better? Not merely through improving grammar or vocabulary.

I aim by teaching students the different variations of communication, showing the importance of tone, volume, postures, gestures, breathing and proximity. Some students are lucky enough to learn some of the above through acting classes and self-development programs but what if schools were to teach all students the real art of communication. I took a course in psychology that also stated the various forms of communication.

Even the way you shake hands with someone is a form of communication. Most entrepreneurs will decide if they want to do business with another merely through a handshake. However, these are things to be taught to all. It has to be part of the curriculum like how algebra is. Imagine what the remarkable outcomes will be. Healthy self-esteem and confidence just are a few, to begin.

The connection is what we all have in common. We all co-exist with not just human beings but merely with nature, the trees, the sea and not to forget the animals. We are of creation that connects to each other. A connection is why we are here. It is what gives purpose and meaning to life. The ability to feel connected is neurobiological. It has been the programming of being a human. Body language is one key aspect of communication, as we all know that speaking takes up seven percentage of communication.

Therefore educators must place great emphasis on teaching the art of body language as well as show how its value-adds to make an impression which is sufficient for any job interview, be it a position for a sales person or a general manager of the company.

So you might ponder what the art of communication is? I am not here to express that you need an accent (although if you do acquire one, kudos to you) or that you got to have a flair for the languages. I mean look at our generation. It has become one where the faith in a student is diminishing. The light in them is not taught to shine outwards. Little does one know how to communicate their way to seek their highest truth. I mean to take responsibility for guiding students to engage in prompt mediation and scientific prayer. I have discussed meditation earlier so I will move forward to scientific prayer.

It is a term that I learned from the book, the power of your subconscious mind by Dr. Joseph Murphy. Institutions must more or less prescribe it as a guidebook for all students. It can help students learn the depths of their minds. It can help them realise that their mind is the only thing that requires real maneuvering in their life. It could be a powerful tool for better mental and physical communication.

The subconscious mind as defined by Malim & Birch (1998, p. 205), is "one level below conscious awareness". When we try to understand how the learning takes place in the subconscious mind, Fregger (2002) believes that inspiration, insight, and realization all spring from the 'subconscious.'

The subconscious mind is also very sensitive to our thoughts. Our thoughts and emotions can often guide the way the subconscious mind flows. It then can be used to our advantage if we feed our subconscious mind with positive thoughts. If we can learn how to communicate with our minds, we will be able to flow better regarding creativity, intuition, and inspiration. For example, say you are going to give a speech to a large audience, and your conscious mind is panicking. Thoughts like "you are going to fail" can come up.

If you understand the subconscious mind, you can then reaffirm to your mind that you are going to rock that stage or even ask the negative voice to shut up. If you keep on mastering the art of communication toward your subconscious mind, you can then adapt quickly to any situation.

It is almost like being best friends with your mind. A best friend that you can instantly contacts when you are in need. Hence, next time if you want to achieve anything in life, be in union with your subconscious mind. It can change your destiny. If more students were to know this, they could apply it to their institutions, to stop hating on the fact that they are not able to do well in examinations or give an excellent presentation in class. They can instead, try to work it out mentally which is a great form of communication.

The human mind is more complex that we think yet we often fall into patterns and programs that could be for the better or worse. We live in a world where people are manipulated to feed the corporate greed system, and they know how to push the buttons of our monkey brains. The truth is that we are becoming more and more immune to this manipulation. What we need is to learn the tools of the mind, to achieve and manifest our desires. We have to allow our mind to work for us in a way that makes us certain individuals where we do not let others perception exploit our capabilities.

Neuro-linguistic programming

One of such tools we can use that will help train our brain better to be better communicators will be Neuro-Linguistic Programming. I went to an introductory workshop on NLP and was mind blown to see the positive possibilities that came out of it.

Neuro-linguistic programming (NLP) is the groundbreaking study of the process of human thinking. In other words, it is the study of what goes on in our brain when we think. It is where you learn the language of your mind.

Richard Bandler co-created the neuro-linguistic programming, a methodology as a means to understand successful behaviours. It is created to know the difference in thought patterns between those who are successful in life as compared to those who are not. He created techniques to re-design limited old beliefs and ideas and re-engineer the mental system. He believes it is also a way to organize our subjective consciousness.

It is not hard to believe that the way you communicate to your brain could either have positive or adverse effects. For example, say you are in your classroom, and your teacher is talking about the failing rates of the past years. You will for sure start seeing the picture in your head and fear is build up in the room.

It might not be necessary that you are a weak student but just hearing about others failing can set you up for failure. Hence it is important to feed our minds with positive pictures.

Neuro Linguistic Programming then comes into place to help people to think in a way that could help them master their mind. Neuro Linguistic is not a new age phenomenon. It is not a repair mechanism either. It is a tool to optimize the human potential. In fact, NLP is prevalent in the UK school systems. Institutions are growing in countries like Japan, South Korea, and Malaysia.

This technique has helped thousands of people with psychiatric conditions, phobias, allergies or even procrastination. NLP uses the Kinesthetic, Auditory and Visual elements in creating methods. It has been used in businesses, management and is used to train personal coaches and athletes around the world.

Most of us live inside our heads that are self-created. By understanding this, we can then further understand ourselves and the people around us. It helps to figure out what we do want and what we want to avoid in life. NLP include activities that people can do and use on a daily basis to retrain their brain to be of advantage and serve them. Imagine if schools were to hire NLP practitioners. Students can get access to such activities that are often short (10-15minutes) which they could practice daily as part of the curriculum. It could positively affect the behaviours and performance of students.

Chapter 7

A look into the system of my homeland

I was born and raised in Singapore. I have managed to discover the gaps in the public system while journeying through it for twelve years. For a very extended period, I suppressed my intuition into believing that meritocracy is the way of life. I mention meritocracy as that is the policy that rules the lives of Singaporeans. I believed till up to the age of eighteen that I had to sloth away to sustain a living. I thought I had to be intellectually brilliant through my performance in standardized examinations. If I could not attain the merits than failure is the label that my society will kindly present to me.

I studied in public schools all my life and got to experience a sweet tinge of education in a convent school as what Singaporeans will call an elite school. I am immensely grateful for having had great experiences and learning throughout. What is then the issue you may ask? The gaps in the system are very subtle that it takes a magnifying glass to analyze. There is only one-way to better living. It is the hidden message behind the system that our government has framed for us. You see it is true that Singapore claims to have an education route for all. That after the secondary school phase when you have taken the national O'level examinations, there is junior college path that the academically strong could take, the Polytechnic path that provides various courses and the Institute of Technical Education for the vocational students.

After which one could get a chance to get a university education. Although Singapore creates alternate routes, it all keeps crawling back to a white paper qualification that matters in the end. This system could be damaging to the actual potential of a human being.

Singapore is considered to be one of the best places to receive a quality education when you set up only one means of success to society. It instantaneously creates a culture of fear. A fear-inducing system is a propelling force towards failure. It is very true to say that Singaporeans are always fearful of losing out. It is evident in the way we behave. Doing academically well in school have become more of a status maintenance than authentic learning. Singaporeans invest way too much money in tuition apart from school and assessment books. We spend so much money on ten-year series (an assessment book that consists of examination papers from the past ten years) just to get an A grade.

Education is a fundamental need in a country like Singapore. How can we make it accessible to everyone if it is so expensive? A solution could be free education for all. It is not too much to ask as various other governments have adopted such an approach. In fact, Norway a country that is very similar to Singapore regarding having one of the highest gross domestic product per capita and higher prices of goods provide education at no cost.

The Norwegian government says the "the Norwegian government considers access to higher education for all to be an important part of the Norwegian society. Thus, there are usually no tuition fees at state universities and university colleges in Norway." Furthermore, the Norwegian government provides free education to international students regardless of their nationality. It is a sure sign that Singapore could implement the same. Students in Singapore have to fork out thousand of dollars on a university education.

Singapore on the surface reflects as having one of the largest concentrations of billionaires, not every Singaporean is born with a silver spoon. In fact, there are many struggling to afford a higher education. The poverty rate in Singapore is at a high twenty-eight percentage as compared to countries like Malaysia, Australia and the United States of America. This solution will not only ease the burden of debt and financial crisis for students and their families. It will help eradicate economic inequality in the long run. It is not fair for students to invest in education, and live in a gamble situation. I have heard of horror stories from friends in university that some of them do not even get entitled to lecturers who are willing to teach well and to top it off have to ballot for classes. It does make sense for students to have pay so much tuition fees to go through an unsatisfying curriculum that does not benefit them. I am not blaming all lecturers, as I do know of a few who do their best to help their students.

I also believe there is another issue in the funding of education. Statistics from world development indicators shows how Singapore spends the lowest percentage of gross domestic product on education. The problem to note is whether they money received is distributed evenly to Singaporeans.

One other issue is the pupil-teacher ratio, where the parliaments update states that there is one teacher to every eighteen students. However, when you look into a typical classroom, you will be able to see that there is clearly twice the number of students. It then causes students to have less interaction time with teachers that could dampen their progress. I am in no place to condemn the government. I am no politician. In fact, Singapore is labeled to offer a high-class education and it is foolish if I were to say that is no freedom in our choices to pick. No one has the courage to talk about the stigma in a society based on these decisions. All I am seeking is a system that will be more holistic and humanistic.

At the same time, Singapore did make progress with the development of the FutureSchools@Singapore programme. It is a collaboration with Infocomm Development Authority of Singapore (IDA) and Ministry of Education (MOE) to integrate Infocomm technology into the educational model designed for innovative pedagogies and flexible learning environment.

The purpose of this program is to make sure students have adequate skills to face the digital workplaces of the future. Currently, there are seven schools selected to participate in this programme. It is great news for the students studying in the seven schools. What about the rest of the student population? It is essential to create programmes that are inclusive. Handpicking some schools cause an imbalance in the system.

An inclusive education system can cause students to be more tolerant and accept others.

In contrast will be the education system in Finland. It is considered to be one of the top education systems in the world. It has no tuition fee system like Norway that I mentioned earlier. The teacher-student ratio is 1:7. Streaming only begins when students turn 16 instead of 9 here in Singapore. The system also scrapped all the private school to be publicly funded in the 1970s whereas private schools are successful businesses here in Singapore. I can go on about the many wonders of the system in Finland.

However what struck me while researching was how all schools in Finland are equal in standards and is all good schools. There is no superiority. No silently thrashing of schools that are not as good as the ones that are considered to be the top here in Singapore. In simple terms, there is no unhealthy ego and competing. It shows how everyone can do well regardless of which school they studied. It makes the system positive in the sense that there everyone is given a fair opportunity to succeed.

Singapore runs on meritocracy. It is a policy where it allows people to earn from how well they perform. It is still not a fair policy as not all students get the same opportunities to showcase their talent. A student can be brilliant in nature but might not have had the finance to study in a school that offers a better curriculum than a regular school. As I previously mentioned that not all schools are equal here. Since there is a gap in the exposure to learn more, they might end up performing mediocre not being able to reach their full potentials.

I do understand that the issues here are not comparable to the fact that many children in the world are not able to receive a primary education. I am very privileged to have had an education when I know that many others my age have had not even had the opportunity to go to a school. If education offered here become truly fair more people can fight their insecurities and attain peace with them. Then more of us can collaborate to help the real needs of the world. For instance, we can build schools in developing countries if we could just put our differences aside. It will help them to focus on real issues and not worry about whether they are going to end up in a good school.

Chapter 8

Sharings from the world

As I was abroad for my volunteering project engaging with internationals, it struck me that I have to be able to hear their perspectives. I mean getting a global perspective will undoubtedly enrich my discussion I thought. After mustering some courage, I decided to tell my friend, Eunice, from Mexico during one of the tea breaks about the idea of this book. I was so nervous about the idea of sharing a different issue. To my surprise, she went on to agree with my viewpoints and even offered to help me write about the system in her country. Her boyfriend, Enrique, a former professor who worked in Universidad TecMilenio, Chihuahua campus shared his thoughts and the following will be his very words on the system in Mexico.

Some ideas about education in México, by The Salomon Family.

Education in México as in many other countries comes along with income, employment and the guideline of governments and takes a lot of time to give results. On the other hand, the world is changing very fast, and technology is becoming the main issue nowadays.

México´s public education has been kidnapped by politics in which the ruling party has been responsible for the poor results and outcome of students and education systems in our country. Education has to be thought as long-term tasks and by long term, we mean 2 or 3 generations. Therefore we must start now.

The education union in México is the largest one in Latin America and its run by incredibly corrupt leaders who are more worried about gaining political and economic power that doing their job which is educating the kids and youngsters of our country. Private education is quite expensive and unaffordable for more than half of the population. This type of teaching is clearly orientated towards making its graduates businesspeople and providing labor to large enterprises. Also is worth mentioning that these universities are quite profitable. They are managed according to their own interests, which are to make profits, sometimes without having a real interest in the student and country's future. Many graduates end up working in an entirely different work field that the one were trained to do earning low wages.

México´s universities have a fragile budget to finance research and development departments. Therefore, we must import education models from other countries. Education hasn't incorporated the native who are very wealthy in costumes and traditions, and they are being set apart from this learning model.

Results are indigent because there isn't an integrated project that unifies private and public education towards a common goal: to form better and more skilled citizens. Education has to come together with many other reforms: political, social, and economic.

It has to continuously be monitored and aligned with the changes in the world. The foundation for education must be to teach students about civism, respect to animals, nature, and humanity. From what they have shared, I can say that gaps in the system are not subjected to one single country.

I also managed to get another perspective from my friend Joan Kabche, from Lebanon whom I met during the trip to give her opinions. Joan Kabche is a nutritionist who graduated from the University of Balamand and these are what she had to say. The Lebanese educational system is divided into two sectors: private schools and universities, for which there is a charge for admission, and public (government) schools and universities that are practically free of charge. This system is well developed and reaches all levels of the population. Lebanon maintained this advanced educational system structure by well training its teachers before the conflict.

Beirut, the Lebanese capital, served as an educational center for the region; however, this system suffered heavy damage during the civil war but has still survived. The methods of instruction used in Lebanese classrooms are mostly traditional.

Teachers spend lots of time lecturing, giving homework and reading assignments to students, and correcting exercises completed in the classroom. Students play a passive role in the instruction process.

They listen quietly to their teacher, rarely question what is presented, and copy material dictated by the teacher, who uses textbooks as primary sources of instruction. Later on, oral recitation by students is used for grading purposes. Memorization of facts and events is greatly emphasized in Lebanese schools, especially for the purpose of passing external formal exams. Therefore, it is not unusual to see standard answers given to questions on official examinations because certain teachers require their students to memorize model answers for the certain topic.

Implementation of new ideas and methods has been hampered by the lack of adequate educational facilities and well-trained professionals in that regard. *"Growing up in a pretty much conservative country, I was always pressured by my parents to go to school and then to college. It's like I never had a say on whether I wanted to go to college. It was something forced on me and I had no way to escape from it. I still remember the first day I went with my mom to school the principle was so nice they even had an aquarium of fish in front of the entry I think that was there way to calm the kids and making fall in love with the school which is very unlikely to happen."* From what Joan had kindly contributed, you can see the pattern of how the school is purely exam-based.

Standardized examinations, standard answers and if you have anything new to say, then you are an outcast. Not to mention how there is again a lack of facilities and professionals to guide the students. I think the issues with universities are very real and they are global. It is time for a divine intervention. It is the time that the curriculum is shaped for the right of the individual and the planet itself.

Afterword

These days, the motivation of school is leaning towards infesting the mind of a student with fear, lack, competition and scarcity. More and more students who graduate out of the system find themselves trapped in a rat race. There is no real learning taking place within the four walls. Most students go to school aimlessly to make their parents proud or with an aim to attain financial freedom. Either way, they are being manufactured to please the economy growth of the country. I believe we all want to be happy when we grow up, not be in debt due to student loans. We were all born not just to find jobs and pay bills. We are all souls that have a purpose in life. We are here to help one another grow our potential and elevate humanity. We are all here to contribute to the wellness of our earth and not destroy the heck out of it for the greed of money. We all know that our planet is in a state of despair. We cannot just be ignorant and feed our selfish needs. In the end, it will leach back on us. Spirituality must be addressed within the modern era and taught in schools.

Incorporating simple tools like meditation, visualisation, and theories of the subconscious mind and psychology in the curriculum and making it accessible to every student is necessary. These are more important to health and wellness of the individual. If the person is well, as a whole will the system prosper and head towards a better future for the society.

There is an oneness of all energetic beings. What is lacking though is the ignorance towards humanity. Schools and private publishing companies emphasize more on assessment books and practice papers but really if students are expected to perform better, you have to reinforce about nutrition and adequate sleep.

Education on nutrition and health are available to students, but it often does not elaborate about good health. Merely talking about protein, fats, and carbohydrates and getting exercise is not enough. One needs education on lifestyles such as veganism. Whether the student chooses to pick it up or not is another issue, but it is essential schools raise awareness about veganism in school. Education has to evolve to make changes to push humanity forward through technological and spiritual means.

All that I have written might sound like honey, poetry to the ears of our dear students. However, this is more based on the solutions for our educators. They could consider including the above in the curriculum and reassess what they have prepared for our generation Y and see if it brings about any massive change in the lifestyle of the student learning and the impacts it has on the world.

With that, I have mentioned all that I have to say. I am not a Ph.D. holder or one of the old men who have had all the life experiences and wisdom to share. I am not even a professional in the education system. I am simply a writer with courage. A plain Jane, who analyzes the system and has the courage to critique it. I could just be like everyone else and abide by the rules. However, if I keep suppressing my thoughts and feelings,

I know very well that I will end up with a mental disease or two. I have a right amount of self-love not to let that happen. I am prepared to handle whatever comes after this and that I will continue seeking the truth and raise awareness about things that matter.

Bibliography

1. Achor, S. (2010). The happiness advantage: The seven principles of positive psychology that fuel success and performance at work. New York: Broadway Books.
2. Popham, J. W., (1999). Using standards and assessments. *Why Standardized Tests Don't Measure Educational Quality, 56, 8-15.*
3. Lakhotia, S. (2012). Miracles of health and happiness. New Delhi: Diamond Pocket Books.
4. Ortner, N. (2013). The tapping solution: A revolutionary system for stress-free living. Carlsbad, CA: Hay House.
5. Lennon, J., Harrison, G., & Prabhupāda, A. C. (1983). Chant and be happy: The power of mantra meditation. Los Angeles: Bhaktivedanta Book Trust.
6. Ngerng, Roy (2013, November 21) *How Is Singapore's Education System Unequal?* Retrieved from https://thehearttruths. com/2013/11/21/how-is-singapores-education-system-unequal/
7. Ngerng, Roy (2013, October 28) *Poverty in Singapore Grew from 16% in 2002 to 28% in 2013* Retrieved from https:// thehearttruths.com/2013/10/28/poverty-in-singapore-grew-from-16-in-2002-to-28-in-2013/
8. Sheldon, Christie (2016) *Meet Christie Sheldon* Retrieved from http://www.loveorabove.com/about/christie-sheldon
9. Brown, Brene (2010) *The power of vulnerability Retrieved from* https://www.ted.com/talks/brene_brown_on_vulnerability?language=en
10. https://www.youtube.com/watch?v=meLbMg7ySU4

Ministry of Education (2012) *Media Release* Retrieved from https://www.moe.gov.sg/media/press/files/2012/11/annex-1-factsheet-on-futureschools.pdf

11. Bandler, Richard (2016) Retrieved from http://richardbandler.com

12. Kiyosaki, R. T. (2011). Rich dad poor dad.

13. Hay, L. L. (1987). You can heal your life. Santa Monica, CA: Hay House.

14. Christie, Karen; Durr, Patricia; and Wilkens, Dorothy, "Close-up: Contemporary deaf filmmakers" (2006)http://scholarworks.rit.edu/cgi/viewcontent.cgi?article=1600&context=article

15. Friedman,Thomas(2013,January29)*It'sP.Q.andC.Q.asMuch as I.Q* Retrieved from http://www.nytimes.com/2013/01/30/opinion/friedman-its-pq-and-cq-as-much-as-iq.html

16. Salovey, Peter (n.d.) *Emotional Intelligence* Retrieved from http://www.unh.edu/emotional_intelligence/EIAssets/EmotionalIntelligenceProper/EI1990%20Emotional%20Intelligence.pdf

17. Uhrmacher, Bruce (n.d.) *Uncommon Schooling: A Historical Look at Rudolf Steiner, Anthroposophy, and Waldorf Education* Retrieved from http://lchc.ucsd.edu/MCA/Mail/xmcamail.2010_01.dir/pdfx9STo74Xyx.pdf

18. MindValley (n.d.) *The 3 Most Important Questions to Ask Yourself* Retrieved from http://www.mindvalley.com/goal-setting-redefined

19. Winn, D. (1983). The manipulated mind: Brainwashing, conditioning, and indoctrination. London: Octagon Press.

20. Gawain, S. (2002). Creative Visualization: Use the Power of Your Imagination to Create What You Want in Your Life. New World Library.

21. Stanford Encyclopedia of Philosophy (2004, Nov 30) *Quantum Approaches to Consciousness* Retrieved from http://plato.stanford.edu/entries/qt-consciousness/

22. American Psychological Association (2011) *What Are the Benefits of Mindfulness? A Practice Review of Psychotherapy-Related Research* Retrieved from **https://www.apa.org/pubs/journals/features/pst-48-2-198.pdf**

23. Transcendental Meditation (n.d.) Retrieved from **http://transcendental-meditation.sg**

24. PNAS (2010) *Prefrontal cortex mediation of cognitive enhancement in rewarding motivational contexts* Retrieved from **http://www.pnas.org/content/107/19/8871.abstract**

25. **https://www.youtube.com/watch?v=TR8TjCncvIw**

26. Britton, Willoughly (2014, June 15) *The Messy Truth About Mindfulness* Retrieved from **http://www.mindful.org/willoughby-britton-the-messy-truth-about-mindfulness/**

27. Goleman, Daniel (2013) *Emotional Intelligence* Retrieved from **http://www.emotionalintelligencecourse.com/eq-history/**

28. University of Rochester Medical Centre (2016) Retrieved from **https://www.urmc.rochester.edu/encyclopedia/content.aspx?ContentTypeID=1&ContentID=3051'**

29. **https://www.youtube.com/watch?v=nhcsPVLAeXU**

30. Ryan, M. J. (1999). Attitudes of Gratitude How to Give and Receive Joy Everyday of Your Life. Newburyport: Red Wheel Weiser.

31. **http://cdp.sagepub.com/content/21/1/54.short**

32. **https://www.youtube.com/results?search_query=shawn+achor**

33. Kondō, M., & Hirano, C. (n.d.). The life-changing magic of tidying up: The Japanese art of decluttering and organizing.

34. Murphy, J. (1963). The power of your subconscious mind. Englewood Cliffs, NJ: Prentice-Hall.

35. Murphy, Joseph (n.d.) *The Power of Subconscious Mind* Retrieved from **http://www.law-of-attraction-haven.com/support-files/power-subconscious-mind.pdf**

36. Stanford Encyclopedia of Philosophy (2003, Aug 19) *Dualism* Retrieved from http://plato.stanford.edu/entries/dualism/

37. Hendrickson, Katie (n.d.) *Assessment in Finland: A Scholarly Reflection on One Country's Use of Formative, Summative, and Evaluative Practices* Retrieved from **http://www.mwera.org/MWER/volumes/v25/issue1-2/v25n1-2-Hendrickson-GRADUATE-STUDENT-SECTION.pdf**

38. Study in Norway (n.d.) **http://www.studyinnorway.no**